THE UNIVERSITY OF
OKLAHOMA®
COOKBOOK

JEN ELSNER

PHOTOGRAPHS BY ZAC WILLIAMS

GIBBS SMITH
TO ENRICH AND INSPIRE HUMANKIND

First Edition
16 15 14 13 12   5 4 3 2 1

Text © 2012 Jen Elsner
Photographs © 2012 Zac Williams

Published by
Gibbs Smith
P.O. Box 667
Layton, Utah 84041

1.800.835.4993 orders
www.gibbs-smith.com

Printed and bound in China

Gibbs Smith books are printed on either recycled, 100% post-consumer waste, FSC-certified papers or on paper produced from sustainable PEFC-certified forest/controlled wood source. Learn more at www.pefc.org.

Library of Congress Cataloging-in-Publication Data

Elsner, Jen.
The University of Oklahoma cookbook / Jen Elsner ;
photographs by Zac Williams. — 1st ed.
p. cm.
ISBN 978-1-4236-3025-8
1. Cooking, American—Southern style.
2. Cooking—Oklahoma.
I. Title.
TX715.2.S68E47 2012
641.5973—dc23
2012009986

CONTENTS

Okra-HOMA

Ingredients

4 to 5 cups vegetable oil

2 eggs, beaten

$3/4$ cup milk

1 cup cornmeal

1 cup flour

$1^1/2$ teaspoons salt

$1/2$ teaspoon pepper

$1/4$ teaspoon cayenne
pepper or $1/2$ teaspoon
crushed red pepper

2 pounds fresh okra,
sliced $1/2$-inch thick

✻ Makes 6–8 servings ✻

Heat oil in a large skillet, preferably cast iron.

In a large bowl, combine the eggs and milk and then stir until well-blended. In a medium bowl, mix cornmeal, flour, salt, and peppers. Add the okra to the egg mixture and stir until evenly coated. Dredge okra in cornmeal-flour mixture to coat well.

Gently add okra to the hot oil with a slotted spoon and cook until golden brown, turning as needed. It is best to fry the okra in batches so that it does not stick together or cook unevenly. Remove from oil, drain on paper towels, and serve immediately.

Touchdown
TATERS

Ingredients

1 bag (32 ounces)
   frozen hash brown
   potatoes, thawed

1 can (10.75 ounces)
   cream of chicken soup

1 cup sour cream

1 cup grated cheddar cheese

1 cup grated Pepper
   Jack cheese

1 cup crushed corn flakes

1 roll Ritz crackers, crushed

1 1/2 teaspoons salt

1/2 teaspoon pepper

1/4 cup melted butter

* Makes about 10 servings *

Preheat oven to 350 degrees and grease a 9 x 13-inch baking dish.

In a large bowl, mix together the potatoes, soup, sour cream, and cheeses. Pour mixture into the prepared baking dish.

In a medium bowl, mix together the corn flakes, cracker crumbs, salt, and pepper. Add the butter and stir to combine. Spread the topping over the potato mixture. Bake for 45 minutes.

Sooner® Pride
POTATO SKINS

Ingredients

6 medium-size
  baking potatoes

3 tablespoons olive oil

1 pound bacon

3 tablespoons vegetable oil

$1/2$ teaspoon salt

$1/8$ teaspoon pepper

$3/4$ cup grated cheddar cheese

$1/4$ cup grated Pepper
  Jack cheese

$1/2$ cup sour cream

2 green onions, sliced,
  including the greens

✱ Makes 12 potato skins ✱

Preheat oven to 400 degrees. Wash the potatoes then rub with olive oil. Bake directly on the oven rack for 1 hour or until the potatoes are cooked through. While the potatoes are cooking, fry the bacon in a large skillet until crispy. Remove the cooked bacon and place onto paper towels to drain. Let cool then crumble.

When the potatoes are done, remove from the oven and let cool for about 10 minutes, or until cool enough to handle. Turn the oven to 450 degrees. Cut the potatoes in half lengthwise. Using a spoon, gently scoop out the insides, leaving about $1/4$ inch of potato on the skin walls. Combine the vegetable oil, salt, and pepper and brush all over the potato skins, inside and out. Place the potatoes on a greased baking sheet or roasting pan. Bake for about 10 minutes face down, then turn the potatoes over on the skin side, and bake for another 10 minutes. Remove from oven.

Sprinkle the insides with the cheeses and crumbled bacon. Broil for 2 minutes, or until the cheese is melted. Transfer the potato skins to a serving tray and top each skin with sour cream and green onions. Serve immediately.

OU®
CHILI PIE

Ingredients

2 pounds ground beef

1 onion, chopped

1 green bell pepper, chopped

1 can (28 ounces) crushed
tomatoes, with liquid

1 can (8 ounces) tomato sauce

2 cans (15 ounces each)
kidney or pinto
beans, drained

1 teaspoon pepper

3 teaspoons chili powder

1 1/2 teaspoons garlic powder

1 teaspoon dried parsley

1 bag (18 ounces) corn chips

2 cups grated cheddar cheese

1 cup grated Colby
Jack cheese

Optional: chopped
onion, diced tomatoes,
shredded lettuce, sliced
jalapenos, sour cream

Cook beef in a large skillet until browned. Place the beef into a slow cooker and add onion, bell pepper, tomatoes, tomato sauce, beans, pepper, chili powder, garlic powder, and parsley. Stir until blended. Cover and cook on low for 6–8 hours or on high for 4 hours.

To serve, place a handful of corn chips in the bottom of individual serving bowls and then cover with chili, cheeses, and optional toppings.

✳ Makes 10–12 servings ✳

Big Red
SMOKIES

Ingredients

1 package (14 ounces) Lit'l Smokies cocktail links

1 cup barbecue sauce

1/2 teaspoon Worcestershire sauce

1 tablespoon jelly of choice (grape or apricot work best)

1 teaspoon packed brown sugar

2 teaspoons ketchup

Place all ingredients into a slow cooker and heat for about 2 hours on high. You can also cook the links on the stovetop in a large saucepan over medium low heat, stirring occasionally so that the sauce doesn't stick to the bottom of the pan, for 30–45 minutes, or until the sauce is thick and bubbly.

✳ Makes about 8 servings ✳

Boomer
BAKED BEANS

Ingredients

2 cans (16 ounces each)
   baked beans with pork

$1/4$ cup chopped onion

$1/4$ cup packed brown sugar

1 tablespoon ketchup

2 tablespoons barbecue sauce

2 teaspoons
   Worcestershire sauce

1 teaspoon mustard

* Makes about 6 servings *

Preheat oven to 350 degrees.

Mix all of the ingredients together in a large bowl and place into a lightly greased 2-quart casserole dish. Cover and bake for 1 hour or until hot and bubbly.

OU®
CHANT AND CHEESE

Ingredients

1 pound macaroni pasta

4 tablespoons butter

1/4 teaspoon flour

3 cups milk

2 slices American cheese, cut into strips

1 cup grated cheddar cheese

1/2 cup grated Colby Jack cheese

1/2 cup grated Pepper Jack cheese

1 teaspoon onion powder

Salt and pepper, to taste

Chopped tomato, optional

* Makes 6–8 servings *

In a large saucepan, cook pasta according to package instructions. Drain in a colander and set aside.

Using the same pan, melt butter and then add the flour, a little at a time, continuously stirring until the mixture is thick and blended, just a couple of minutes. Slowly stir in the milk and allow mixture to thicken. Turn the heat to low and let simmer for 5 minutes.

Place the American cheese strips in the milk mixture, a couple at a time, whisking until melted. Then gradually stir in the rest of the cheeses, 1/2 cup at a time, until all cheeses are melted. Do not use pregrated packaged cheese, as it will not melt properly. Add onion powder and salt and pepper, to taste. Stir in the cooked pasta and mix with the cheese sauce until thoroughly coated.

Place in serving bowls and garnish with tomato, if desired.

Covered Wagon
CHICKEN STRIPS

Ingredients

4 boneless chicken breasts

4 cups milk, divided

Vegetable oil

1 cup plus 4 tablespoons flour, divided

1/2 teaspoon seasoned salt

1/8 teaspoon ground pepper

1/8 teaspoon garlic powder

1/4 teaspoon onion powder

1/2 teaspoon dried parsley

Dash of celery salt

* Makes 4–6 servings *

Rinse the chicken breasts and cut them into 1-inch strips. Place them in a shallow bowl with 2 cups milk. In a large cast iron skillet or heavy frying pan, heat enough oil to cover the bottom, about 1 inch deep.

In a medium bowl, mix together 1 cup flour, seasoned salt, pepper, garlic powder, onion powder, parsley, and celery salt. Transfer the chicken pieces to the flour mixture and toss until thoroughly coated. Once the oil is hot, place the coated chicken into the pan. Fry the strips for about 10 minutes on each side then keep turning the chicken until golden brown. Remove the fried strips from the pan and pat off the excess oil with a paper towel. Cover with aluminum foil to keep warm.

To make gravy, drain all but about 4 tablespoons of oil from the pan. Add 4 tablespoons flour to the drippings and mix into a paste. Add 1 1/2 cups milk, a little at a time. Bring to a boil, stirring continuously. If gravy is too thick, add more milk in small increments. Stir until thickened and smooth. Add extra seasoned salt and pepper, to taste.

Serve chicken strips with gravy on the side.

Land Run
CASSEROLE

Ingredients

1 pound ground beef

1 package taco seasoning

1/2 cup water

1 jar (16 ounces)
   salsa con queso

3 slices American cheese

2 cups grated Colby
   Jack cheese

2 cups grated Pepper
   Jack cheese

1 cup crushed tortilla chips

Chopped green leaf
   lettuce and chopped
   tomatoes, optional

Tortillas chips and
   flour tortillas

* Makes about 8 servings *

Preheat oven to 400 degrees.

In a large skillet, brown beef and drain off the excess grease. Return to stove over medium heat and add taco seasoning and water. Mix until the seasoning is dissolved. Simmer until the liquid is gone, stirring occasionally.

In a deep 9-inch casserole dish, layer the salsa con queso, seasoned beef, cheeses, and crushed tortilla chips. Repeat this layering process until all ingredients are gone. End with cheeses on the top layer. Cover and bake for 45 minutes.

Garnish with lettuce and tomatoes, if desired, and serve with tortilla chips and flour tortillas.

Sooner Magic®
STEAK SANDWICHES

Ingredients

1/3 cup vegetable oil

4 cubed steaks

1 cup milk

2 cups plus 6 tablespoons flour, divided

1 3/4 teaspoons seasoned salt, divided

1/4 teaspoon plus 1/8 teaspoon ground pepper, divided

1/4 teaspoon garlic powder

3/4 teaspoon onion powder, divided

1/2 teaspoon dried parsley

Dash of celery salt

3 cups hot water

1 can (4 ounces) sliced mushrooms, drained

4 onion buns

✳ Makes 4 servings ✳

In a large skillet, warm oil over medium heat to medium-high. Place steaks in a shallow dish with milk and set aside.

In a medium bowl, mix together 2 cups flour, 1 teaspoon seasoned salt, 1/4 teaspoon pepper, garlic powder, 1/2 teaspoon onion powder, parsley, and celery salt. Dredge steaks in the flour mixture until thoroughly coated. Once oil is hot, place the coated steaks into the pan. Fry on each side until browned, about 6–8 minutes on each side. Transfer the steaks from the skillet to a slow cooker.

Over medium-low heat, add 6 tablespoons flour to the drippings in the skillet and stir until browned and well blended. Add water, a little at a time, until the roux has turned into a smooth gravy. Add remaining seasoned salt, pepper, and onion powder and stir to combine. Add mushrooms and stir. Pour the gravy over the steaks and cook in the slow cooker on high, for 2 hours.

Open the buns and place them face-up on a baking sheet. Broil for just a couple of minutes, until toasted. Top with steaks and serve immediately.

Championship CHILI

Ingredients

2 pounds ground beef

1 can (14.5 ounces)
beef broth

1 package taco seasoning

1/4 teaspoon chili powder

1 can (15 ounces) pinto
beans, with liquid

1 can (10 ounces) Rotel
Original Diced Tomatoes
and Green Chiles

3 cups tomato juice (use less
for a thicker consistency)

1 bag (12 ounces) frozen
corn (yellow and white)

1 1/2 to 2 cups grated
cheddar cheese, optional

Crackers or tortilla
chips, optional

✱ Makes 8–10 servings ✱

In a large skillet, cook beef until browned and drain off excess grease.

In a large saucepan or stock pot over medium heat, mix broth, taco seasoning, and chili powder until dissolved. Add beef, beans, and Rotel; stir to combine. Add tomato juice and frozen corn, stirring until evenly mixed. Turn the heat down to medium-low and simmer, stirring occasionally until chili is hot.

Ladle into bowls and top with cheese, if using. Serve with crackers or tortilla chips, if desired.

Sooner®
SLIDERS

Ingredients

1 pork roast (4 pounds)

1 tablespoon liquid smoke

1 teaspoon onion powder

1 teaspoon garlic powder

2 tablespoons
  Worcestershire sauce

$1/2$ teaspoon salt

$1/4$ teaspoon pepper

1 bottle (16 ounces)
  barbecue sauce

12 small slider buns or
  Hawaiian bread rolls

Sliced pickles, optional

* Makes 12 servings *

Place the meat on a piece of aluminum foil large enough to wrap entire roast and season with liquid smoke, onion powder, garlic powder, Worcestershire sauce, salt, and pepper. Wrap the foil around the roast and place in a slow cooker on high for 4 hours, or on low for 7–8 hours.

Remove the roast from the slow cooker and unwrap it. Place the cooked pork on a large plate and use 2 forks to pull it apart into shredded pieces. Place the pulled pork back into the slow cooker and add the barbecue sauce. Cook on high for 10–20 more minutes. Slice open the buns and heap on the pulled pork. Add pickles, if desired.

Schooner
KABOBS

Ingredients

1 can (15 ounces) pineapple chucks

3 cloves garlic, crushed

1/4 cup Worcestershire sauce

1/4 cup plus 1 tablespoon teriyaki sauce

1/4 cup plus 1 tablespoon soy sauce

1/8 teaspoon paprika

1 teaspoon pepper

1/4 teaspoon crushed red pepper

About 1/2 cup pineapple juice

4 chicken breasts, cut into 1-inch cubes

1 red bell pepper, cut into 1-inch chunks

1 red onion, cut into 1-inch chunks

1 pound red potatoes, quartered

Drain pineapple chunks and reserve juice to use in the marinade.

In a large bowl, combine garlic, Worcestershire sauce, teriyaki sauce, soy sauce, paprika, peppers, and pineapple juice. Add the chicken cubes and stir to coat. Seal the bowl with plastic wrap and refrigerate for at least an hour, but do not exceed 5 hours.

On metal skewers, thread bell pepper, onion, chicken, pineapple, and potato. Repeat until skewer is full, leaving 1–2 inches of room on each end. Place the kabobs on a preheated grill, turning every 3–4 minutes for even cooking. Grill until chicken is golden and the inside is no longer pink.

Note: If you use wooden skewers, soak them in water for about 30 minutes before using.

✳ Makes 4–6 servings ✳

RUF/NEK™
MEATLOAF SANDWICHES

Ingredients

1 pound ground beef

1 teaspoon salt

1/2 teaspoon pepper

1 onion, chopped

2 cloves garlic, minced

1 green bell pepper, chopped

1 can (2.25 ounces)
   sliced olives

1 cup quick oats

1/2 cup ketchup, plus
   more, to taste

1 package hamburger buns

✳ Makes 6–8 servings ✳

Preheat oven to 350 degrees.

In a large bowl, combine beef, salt, pepper, onion, garlic, bell pepper, olives, oats, and 1/2 cup ketchup. Mix well and place into a greased 8-inch loaf pan. Cover the top of the loaf with more ketchup, to taste, and bake for 1 hour.

Cut into 1-inch slices and serve on buns.

Oklahoma®
INDIAN TACOS

Ingredients

1 pound ground beef

1 package taco seasoning

1 can (16 ounces) refried beans

1 can (10 ounces) Rotel Original Diced Tomatoes and Green Chiles

Vegetable oil

2 cups flour

3 teaspoons baking powder

1/2 teaspoon salt

1 cup milk

Toppings: shredded lettuce, grated cheddar and Pepper Jack cheeses, diced tomatoes, sour cream, salsa, sliced black olives

In a large skillet, cook the beef until browned; add the taco seasoning mix, following the instructions on the package. When the seasoned beef is done, add the beans and Rotel and stir until well blended. Continue to simmer on low until fry bread is ready.

For the fry bread, place enough oil in another large skillet for deep-frying (about an inch deep) and set it on medium-high heat. While the oil is heating, combine the flour, baking powder, and salt in a large bowl. Slowly pour in the milk while stirring until it makes pliable dough. Pinch off 2–3 inch pieces and work into flat disks on a lightly floured surface. Fry in hot oil for 3–4 minutes on each side or until golden. Remove the fry bread from the skillet and dab off excess grease on paper towels.

To serve, place a large spoonful of the beef mixture on top of the fry bread and garnish with any or all of the toppings.

✱ Makes 4 servings ✱

Victory
VEGGIE PIZZA

Ingredients

- 2 cans (8 ounces each) crescent rolls
- 2 packages (8 ounces each) cream cheese, softened
- 1 cup mayonnaise
- 1 package dry ranch salad dressing mix
- 1 cup chopped broccoli
- 1 cup chopped cauliflower
- 1 cup sliced red bell pepper
- 1 cup diced green bell pepper
- 1 cup shredded carrots
- 1 cup grated cheddar cheese, optional

✳ Makes about 12 servings ✳

Preheat oven to 375 degrees.

Lightly apply nonstick cooking spray to a 10 x 15-inch baking sheet. Roll out the crescent dough onto the baking sheet and pinch the edges together to form a crust. There will be some dough left over. Bake for 12 minutes. Remove from the oven and let cool for 15 minutes.

In a medium bowl, combine the cream cheese, mayonnaise, and ranch dressing mix. Spread the mixture over the cooled crust. Arrange the prepared vegetables over the cream cheese layer and sprinkle the cheese on top, if using.

Chill for 1 hour then slice into 3-inch squares and serve.

7-Point
SALAD

Ingredients

1 pound bacon

1 cup frozen peas

1/2 cup mayonnaise

1 head iceberg or
   romaine lettuce (or a
   mixture of both)

1 red bell pepper, chopped

2 cups chopped celery

1 tomato, diced

1 cup grated cheddar cheese

1/4 cup chopped chives

1/4 cup vinegar

3/4 cup sugar

✱ Makes about 12 servings ✱

In a large skillet, cook the bacon; remove to paper towels to cool and then crumble. In a small bowl, mix the peas and mayonnaise together.

In individual serving dishes or a large serving bowl, layer the ingredients as follows: lettuce, bell pepper, celery, tomato, pea mixture, cheese, and chives.

In small bowl, mix the vinegar and sugar together then add the bacon and stir. Pour over the top of the salad and serve.

Pioneer
POTATO SALAD

Ingredients

3 pounds red potatoes, unpeeled

4 eggs

3/4 cup chopped onion

1 cup chopped celery

2 teaspoons paprika

1/2 teaspoon garlic powder

1/4 teaspoon pepper

2 tablespoons dried parsley

2 cups mayonnaise

3 teaspoons prepared mustard

Salt, to taste

✳ Makes 10–12 servings ✳

Clean the potatoes and place them in a large pot with enough water to cover. Bring to a boil and cook for about 15 minutes. Drain and set in the refrigerator to cool.

Place eggs in a small saucepan and cover with cold water, about an inch above the eggs. Add a pinch of salt to the water to make the eggs easier to peel. Bring just to a boil and immediately remove from heat. Cover and let the eggs stand in hot water for about 15 minutes. Remove eggs from hot water and cool in a bowl of cold water. Once the eggs have cooled, peel and chop them.

Cut the potatoes into quarters or eighths, depending on desired size, leaving the skin on. Place into a large bowl. Add the eggs, onion, celery, paprika, garlic powder, pepper, and parsley. Blend together. Mix in the mayonnaise and mustard then salt to taste. Cover with plastic wrap and place in the refrigerator for at least an hour before serving.

Go Sooners®
RED PEPPERS AND FIXIN'S

Ingredients

1 cup dried breadcrumbs

3 tablespoons grated
   Parmesan cheese

1 teaspoon garlic powder

1 teaspoon salt

$1/4$ teaspoon pepper

1 egg, beaten

1 tablespoon milk

1 large red bell pepper, sliced

$1^1/2$ cups broccoli florets

1 zucchini, cut into sticks

1 to 2 tablespoons
   butter, melted

* Makes 4–6 servings *

Place wax paper on a baking sheet and set aside.

In a large bowl, combine breadcrumbs, cheese, garlic powder, salt, and pepper. In a small bowl, combine egg and milk. Coat veggies in the egg mixture then transfer them, in small batches, to the breadcrumb blend. Make sure to toss the veggies around to get a good, even coating. Place the coated veggies on the prepared baking sheet and use leftover breading to cover any missed spots. Refrigerate for about 30 minutes—this will help the coating stick to the veggies better.

Preheat oven to 400 degrees and prepare a baking sheet with nonstick cooking spray.

Transfer the veggies to the prepared baking sheet and drizzle with melted butter. Bake for about 20 minutes, or until crisp, stirring gently after 10 minutes of baking time.

Rose Rock
RANCH DIP

Ingredients

1 cup mayonnaise

1/2 cup sour cream

2 tablespoons finely
chopped chives

2 teaspoons finely
chopped fresh dill

1/2 teaspoon dried parsley

1/4 teaspoon garlic powder

1/4 teaspoon onion powder

1/4 teaspoon paprika

Salt and pepper, to taste

Buttermilk, as needed

Cut vegetables,
crackers, or chips

✱ Makes 1 1/2 cups ✱

In a medium bowl, mix together the mayonnaise,
sour cream, chives, dill, parsley, garlic powder,
onion powder, paprika, salt, and pepper. Use a small
amount of buttermilk to thin out dip to desired
consistency. Cover and refrigerate for 30 minutes to
an hour before serving with cut vegetables, crackers,
or chips.

Sooner Nation®
SALSA

Ingredients

1 lime

8 Roma tomatoes

1/2 cup fresh cilantro

1 clove garlic

1/4 onion

1 jalapeno

3 tablespoons olive oil

1/4 teaspoon salt

Tortilla chips

* Makes about 2 cups *

Half the lime and squeeze the juice from both halves into a food processor. Place all of the remaining ingredients into the food processor. Pulsate until contents are evenly mixed, but still chunky. Spoon into a bowl and serve with tortilla chips.

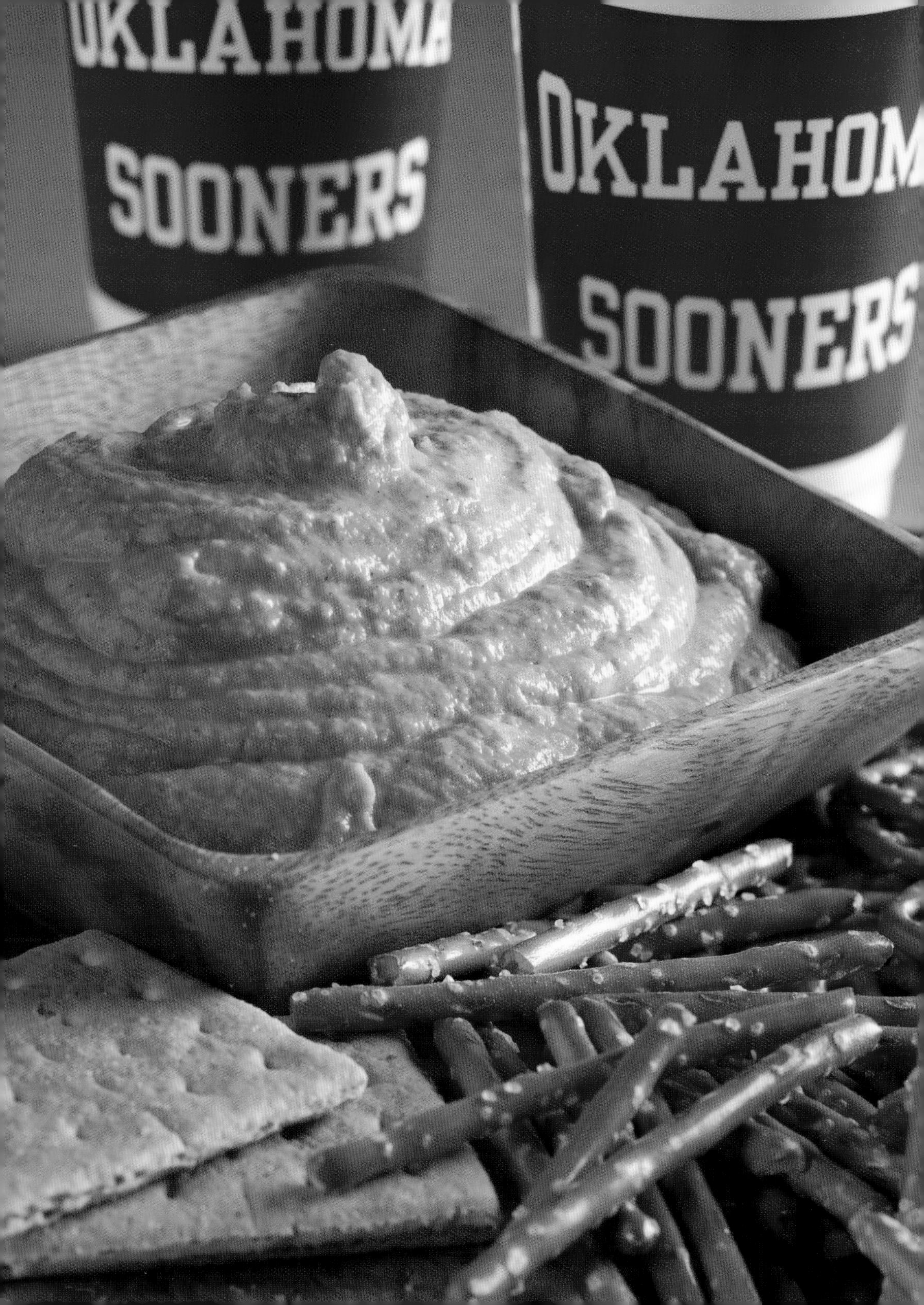
OKLAHOMA
SOONERS
OKLAHOM
SOONERS

Pride of Oklahoma®
PUMPKIN DIP

Ingredients

1 package (8 ounces)
    cream cheese, softened

1 can (15 ounces) pumpkin

1 teaspoon vanilla

1 cup packed brown sugar

1 teaspoon pumpkin
    pie spice

1 teaspoon cinnamon

Graham crackers, ginger
    snaps, and pretzels

✳ Makes about 3 cups ✳

In a large bowl, stir the cream cheese until most of the lumps are gone. Add the pumpkin and vanilla and stir until mixture is smooth and creamy. Blend in brown sugar and spices. Refrigerate until ready to serve.

Pour into a serving bowl and serve with graham crackers, ginger snaps, and pretzels.

Red River
PUNCH

Ingredients

- 1 large box cherry-flavor gelatin
- 3 cups boiling water
- 2 cups sugar
- 1 can (12 ounces) frozen lemonade, thawed
- 5 cups ginger ale
- 1 lemon, sliced, optional

* Makes 20–25 servings *

In a large pitcher or punch bowl, dissolve the gelatin in boiling water; add sugar and stir. Dilute the lemonade as the package instructions suggest and mix in with the gelatin.

Just before serving, add the ginger ale. Add the lemon slices to the pitcher or place on the side of individual serving glasses, if desired.

Crimson and Cream
STRAWBERRY SMOOTHIE

Ingredients

1 cup frozen strawberries

1/4 cup frozen orange juice,
   thawed, but slushy

1 cup milk

1 teaspoon vanilla extract

Ice

Fresh strawberries
   and whipped cream,
   for garnish

✳ Makes 1–2 servings ✳

In a blender or food processor, combine frozen strawberries, orange juice, milk, and vanilla and blend until mixture is smooth and creamy. Add enough ice for desired consistency and blend.

Pour into a tall glass and garnish with a fresh strawberry and whipped cream.

Stormin' Norman
PECAN PIE

Ingredients

3 eggs

1 cup sugar

$1/2$ teaspoon salt

1 cup white corn syrup

1 teaspoon vanilla

$1/4$ cup unsalted
   butter, softened

1 cup chopped pecans

2 (9-inch) unbaked pie
   shells (not deep-dish),
   thawed if frozen

Whipped cream, optional

✱ Makes 8 servings ✱

Preheat oven to 350 degrees.

In a medium bowl, beat the eggs. Add sugar, salt, corn syrup, vanilla, butter, and pecans. Stir until thoroughly mixed. Place the pie shells side-by-side on a baking sheet and distribute the pecan filling evenly between them.

Bake for 50 minutes to an hour, or until crusts are browned. To test if pie is done, stick a butter knife in the center. If it comes out clean, the pie is done, if not, bake for another 10 minutes or so.

Allow to cool and serve slices topped with a dollop of whipped cream, if desired.

Boomer Sooner®
SUGAR COOKIES

Ingredients

4 cups flour

3 teaspoons baking powder

1 teaspoon salt

1 teaspoon nutmeg

1 cup butter-flavor shortening

1 cup sugar

1 cup firmly packed brown sugar

2 tablespoons milk

3 eggs

1 teaspoon vanilla

1 container (12 ounces) whipped vanilla frosting

Red food coloring paste

1 tube (4.25 ounces) red decorator frosting

1 tube (4.25 ounces) white decorator frosting

* Makes about 4 dozen *

Preheat oven to 350 degrees.

Combine flour, baking powder, salt, and nutmeg together in a large bowl; set aside. In another large bowl, cream the shortening by beating on high for about 30 seconds with an electric mixer. Add both sugars and beat until thoroughly mixed, about 2–3 minutes. Add the milk and beat in eggs, one at a time, then add vanilla. Mix until well blended. Slowly add the dry ingredients, mixing by hand until combined.

Divide the dough in half and chill for at least 30 minutes. On a lightly floured surface, roll the dough out to 1/4-inch thick. Cut out helmets with shaped cookie cutters. Place cookies 1 inch apart on lightly greased baking sheets. Bake for 10–12 minutes or until lightly browned. Transfer cookies to a wire rack to cool.

Divide frosting in half and tint one half red using food coloring paste. Decorate half of the cookies with white frosting and pipe an outline onto the cookies with red. Decorate the other half with red frosting and white piping.

Schooner
SHORTBREAD THUMBPRINTS

Ingredients

1 cup butter, softened
$^1/_2$ cup sugar
$2^1/_4$ cups flour
1 teaspoon vanilla
$^1/_2$ cup red jam, of choice

✳ Makes about 2 dozen ✳

Preheat oven to 325 degrees.

Cream the butter and sugar together in a medium bowl. Add the flour and knead with your hands to incorporate. Add vanilla and mix thoroughly. Gather the mixture into a ball and knead until formed into a smooth, soft dough.

Pinch off small portions of the dough and roll into 1-inch balls. Place 1 inch apart on ungreased baking sheets. Lightly press your thumb into the center of each ball and fill the well with $^1/_4$–$^1/_2$ teaspoon jam. Do not overfill. Bake for 20–25 minutes or until the cookies are golden brown.

Redbud
AMBROSIA

Ingredients

1 large box cherry-
   flavor gelatin

1 can (8 ounces) crushed
   pineapple, drained

1 package (8 ounces)
   cream cheese, softened

1 container (8 ounces)
   whipped topping

1 cup chopped walnuts
   or pecans

✱ Makes 8–12 servings ✱

Make the gelatin according to the package
instructions.

In a medium bowl, combine the pineapple,
cream cheese, and whipped topping. Mix in the
prepared gelatin. Add nuts and fold gently until all
ingredients are evenly combined.

Cover with plastic wrap and refrigerate until ready
to serve.

Spirit Squad
CHERRY CRISP

Ingredients

5 cups pitted tart
  red cherries

$^1/_2$ cup sugar

1 tablespoon plus $^1/_4$ teaspoon
  cinnamon, divided

2 tablespoons cornstarch

$^1/_2$ cup oats

$^3/_4$ cup packed brown sugar

$^1/_4$ cup plus 3
  tablespoons flour

1 teaspoon allspice

$^1/_3$ cup butter, softened

$^1/_4$ cup chopped nuts

* Makes 6 servings *

Preheat oven to 375 degrees.

In a large bowl, mix the cherries, sugar, 1 tablespoon cinnamon, and cornstarch together; pour into a greased 2-quart baking dish.

In a medium bowl, combine the oats, brown sugar, flour, remaining cinnamon, and allspice. Add the butter in chunks and combine with hands until the mixture resembles coarse crumbs. Add in the nuts. Spread the topping evenly over the fruit.

Bake for 30 minutes or until filling is bubbly and the topping is golden.

Note: You can make individual servings by using 6 ramekins and reducing the baking time by about 10 minutes.

Spiced
FOOTBALLS

Ingredients

3 cups whole almonds

2 tablespoons butter

1 teaspoon cinnamon

**$1/2$ teaspoon pumpkin
pie spice**

$1/2$ teaspoon allspice

✱ Makes 3 cups ✱

In a large skillet, toast almonds over medium heat for about 8 minutes, stirring occasionally. Remove almonds and set aside.

In the same pan, melt butter then add the spices. Stir the mixture around for a couple of minutes, letting the flavors blend together, then turn heat to low. Add the almonds back into the pan, stirring until evenly coated.

JEN ELSNER has a passion for cooking and hosting game-day parties. She has a Masters Degree in Professional Writing from the University of Oklahoma and works for the university's English Department. She lives in Norman, Oklahoma.